I Left Myself Behind

I Left Myself Behind

A Selection of Poems and Prose Dedicated to Abused Women

Carol Samuels

iUniverse, Inc.
Bloomington

I Left Myself Behind
A Selection of Poems and Prose Dedicated to Abused Women

iUniverse books may be ordered through booksellers or by contacting:

iUniverse
1663 Liberty Drive
Bloomington, IN 47403
www.iuniverse.com
1-800-Authors (1-800-288-4677)

ISBN: 978-1-4759-7287-0 (sc)
ISBN: 978-1-4759-7286-3 (hc)
ISBN: 978-1-4759-7285-6 (e)

Library of Congress Control Number: 2013901353

Printed in the United States of America

iUniverse rev. date: 01/25/2013

Table of Contents

DEDICATION ix

INTRODUCTION xi

Section I: Reflections 1

1–LOVE NO POWER WITHOUT 3

2–WHAT DO I SEE 4

3–DAUGHTERS OF THE WORLD 7

4–HOW DO YOU FEEL 10

5–LIGHT IN THE DARKNESS 12

6–IT STANDS TO REASON MY DEAR 14

7–DELICIOUS BUDDIES MAKE ME SMILE 15

8–COLD 17

9–BEGINNING OF THE END 18

10–TODAY 20

11–LONELY 22

12–THE BEAUTY OF NO PAIN - HAPPINESS 25

13–A FRIEND FOR THE NIGHT 27

14–MELANCHOLY 29

15–EGO TRIPPING 31

16–JUST OUT HAVING A DRINK 34

17–AND THE MOON REMAINS 36

18–THE LAST LAUGH OR A COMICAL TRAGEDY 37

19–I LEFT MYSELF BEHIND 40

20–TO DO OR NOT TO DO 43

21–SKIN. 45

22–ROOTS...STEP OUTTA THE TRAP 47

23–IF YOU LOVE ME. 52

24–WHY I LOVE YOU 53

25–GET GROUNDED. 56

26–DON'T DO IT. 57

27–THIS TOO SHALL PASS - GROWING PAINS 59

28–LET IT BE 61

Section II: Life 63

29–LIFE 65

30–LET THERE BE MEANING TO LIVING 66

31–LIFE...IT'S JUST SOUP 69

32–ME MYSELF AND I AM 71

33–I KEEP MY EYES ON HEAVEN 76

34–CAN'T FIND NO REASON NOT TO LOVE YOU 79

35–HOW WE SURVIVE. 82

36–CAN'T WAIT 83

37–THREE LITTLE WORDS 87

38–WHERE ARE YOU ...WHERE ARE AM I. 91

39–DAY AND NIGHT. 93

40–NO LIFE / SUICIDE 94

41–AN EXTENSION OF HIS PERFECTION. 96

42–NO THINGS WON'T BE THE SAME 98

43–THE GREATEST FIND....NEVER LOST 101

Section III: Thoughts of Healing 105

44–TO KNOW ONESELF 107

45–DO WHAT YOU FEEL 108

46–GETTING THERE 110

47–THE RE-CREATION OF LIFE 113

48–REHABILITATION ...LEARNING TO WALK AGAIN 116

49–SMELLING MY OWN COFFEE 118

50–EYES ON THE FUTURE, LET NO HURDLE BE DISARMING 120

GLOSSARY 123

INDEX 125

Dedication

*Thanks to the persons that inspire me most my loving
parents, my brothers George, James,*

*my children Monifa, Konata, Nataki, Brittany,
Marcus, Dean, and dear husband Robert*

*may be blessed with peace, harmony success, prosperity
and perfect health of body and mind*

*These poems, prose, and thoughts are dedicated to abused women
their mountains, hurdles and challenges...their family and friends
that suffer with and for them...*

Introduction

There, truly is no words that express depth of feelings, just as there is some pain that cannot be smoothed, so we redefine it as mountains we climb, challenges we face and hurdles we jump in the life we live. *I Left Myself Behind* is to abused women around the world with the need to understand the extent we all try to satisfy the need for affection, attention, appreciation or just acknowledgment, positive or negative by the opposite sex. "Daughters of the World" helps us to understand these feelings that many times are misconstrued as you filling a need with the abuser or you being needed by or deserve to be abused by the abuser. Do not get tricked by his "Ego Tripping"... thus justifying "The Last Laugh or This Comical Tragedy".

I Let Myself Behind is divided into three sections; "Reflections", a look at what one is doing (not so much as looking back), "Life" which is about living, and "Thoughts of Healing" which is moving in positive directions and helps us to reflect on the steps we take to go through life and deal with the trials and tribulations of relationships. Some relationships are excellent others have their ups and downs. Still some relationships are filled with abuse verbally, mentally and physically. They exist only to make the abuser or abused value or devalue ones self worth. We try to make everyone happy but realize we sometimes suffer in the process and sacrifice ones own self esteem. In the poem "Beginning of the End"... love and pain are not the same and not the name of the game.. love and affection are just that love and affection never to be compared with hurt and pain, use and abuse.

I Left Myself Behind helps us to realize we need to know ourself and also need to forgive ourself such as in the poems, ("Know Oneself", and "Get Grounded") once doing that we can then begin to re-create our lives into more fulfilling lives. You will then appreciate the poem "Re-creation of Life".

Life is lessons, and we must understand them in order to continue to move forward and grow with positive energy. Your mantra should be "Smelling My Own Coffee". Do not put too much trust in man against your own life and safety. We are all God's children, and we must trust the Most High and move and have our being in faith that we deserve to be happy and treated properly. Until we learn that we will suffer needlessly and call it love, which it is not. God did not bring us here to suffer but to be happy and live abundantly. We forget that and choose to suffer which is against our own existence as expressed in the poem "Roots". Wake up and realize you deserve the best. Anyone treating you less is not providing you what you deserve, the best!

Enjoy the poems "Delicious Buddies Make Me Smile", "Melancholy" and "The Beauty of no Pain". Remember life is also about self-preservation so save your own life by putting you first then others. *I Left Myself Behind* is to the many sweeties that are only looking for a little love attention and affection. It expresses the extent that they will go to and the amount of damage they incur. Not to say they are wrong or right but to ask them to be strong and get along with their life via stepping out of their strife. *Enjoy!*

Section I: Reflections

words to my wife

1–<u>*LOVE NO POWER WITHOUT*</u>

Describe love by the softness of it's curves not the angles of its square corners,

not the pain not the sorry...for love is not there or here or anywhere that has

rough edges it soothes, smoothes...it's not to protest you, molest, abuse, lose,

booze, snooze or groove you...drain, de-brain,de-fame nor claim, frame or push

its insane on you... for love is clarity...no blindness, nor darkness...but light,

beauty, truth, comfort, gladness...giving shelter from the rain/pain and the

insane of society. it is the brightness at the end of the tunnel...it is the

fearlessness of the escape, it is the quench of the thirst, the cool of the breeze,

the heat to the fire, the smell of the magnolia, the twinkle of the star, the cure

of the dis-ease, the flight of the hummingbird,the ripple of the water, the taste

of the dessert or the evolution of life...no hell just happiness, it is the coming of

the next moment/second in time, it is the opening of the flower's petals...

it is the purring of the cat, it is the whistling of the wind in the tree

branches...the flickering sunlight through the leaves, the release of the breath

on the exhale, the calm that defies the storm...the I am of the I am...

the power within since there is no power without

that is the love our marriage is about...

words to my husband

2–<u>WHAT DO I SEE</u>

What do I see when I see you... beauty from the floor up, fabulous from the head

down, soft warm moist breezes floating across the calm clear blue water, dew

drops dripping down blades of tall grass reflecting sunlight like diamond facets

shimmering, sparkling, glistering, dancing, romancing...

while gently you caress the air as you move through the space between

us...commanding justified attention as you shower your essence on the world

like spring rain bouncing and pacing on a dirt road, splashing more dust then

water ...you focusing on both where you came from and where you are going

with a mind actively a buzz like bees on a honey comb...I see the scent of a man

and the salt of your perspiratiion and think of the dill in pickles, the tartness of

cransberries with the aroma of musk over taking both of us...

what do I see when I see you...the tulip opens and soak in the sun drinking its

warmth and light...a snowflake melting changing, evolving to whence it

came...soft drip of water in a warm open pink palm rapidly evaporating...the

sting of a bee and the delayed itch of a mosquito bite...summer moving toward

the beauty of fall, the hot and cold of it all...

what do I see when I see you... with closed eyes the rainbows, the pot of gold, the

eyes of the soul, green grass as we bask in the sun making wishes on the moon

with climaxes too soon...the loud drumming of the clock with its tick-tock

spaced decades apart, time running in endless space...wild flowers tamely,

uniformly growing in the garden of life, splashes of brilliant colors together side by side respecting, loving, complimenting each other united in distinctly

unique beauty as the perfume of life...candles burning, flames flickering,

ringlets of smoke escaping to heaven, kids playing in the park, loud smiles, quiet

laughter, people going nowhere everywhere...warming ice to get cold water...

what do I see when I see you... the light, the darkness, the top of the hill...love

don't kill, we are ad infinitum since we became an item with the sun on the

horizon...eutopia that is you to me...that is what I see... you and me...

3–_DAUGHTERS OF THE WORLD_

Daughters of the world...

stop the fight and live the life you are meant to have/live

daughters!!! the world screams behind dry tears...

stop the fight... the fight for your father's love.

the fight for your father's approval

stop the tears, loud laughter, over eating, over dressing, over working,

over sleeping, over doing, over drugging...

all that you do to get love, appraisal and approval from the father/man you

love

stop looking for love in all the wrong places... in all the wrong people

who have you over working, over eating, over doing, over drugging...

there ain't enough painkillers and vitamins to quiet the pain

not enough food to fill the hunger, not enough water to drown the

sorrow, not enough sleep to erase the tired, not enough pretty in your dressing

for him to see the beauty, not enough tears to quell the fears, not enough

laughter for the funny to shield your fate, not enough strength to hide your

weakness, not enough work to ever get his applaud, appraisal, and approval...

there is never enough giving while you're still living and your dying won't

keep him from lying...

cause he can't give, cause he don't recognize

cause he don't appreciate, cause he don't respect,

cause he don't believe, cause he don't feel

because he don't see the good, he don't see the beauty,

he don't see the love, he don't see the light, he don't see the lord

but you have the love of the one father that brought you here...

the Most High made you daughters of the world...

the backbone of humanity, the building blocks of life,

the carrier of child, the nurturer...the appraiser,

the teacher... the enthusiast, the lover ... the encourager

the mother... the beauty, the good... the positive,

the worker ... the healer, the giver ... the forgiver

stop the fight for your father's love, appraisal and approval

I applaud you ...I celebrate you, I understand you

I love you ...I respect you...I ... your inner self am the real you

I hold my hand out to you, to bring you up ...to encourage you

to stop the fight and live the life you are meant to have

the faith... the confidence, the love ... the hope,

the trust... the intellect,

the spirit... the wit, the laughter...

the joy of a job well done

the love of life...the blue of the sky

the wet of water...the twinkle of stars

the smell of flowers...the taste of honey

the sparkle of diamonds...the laughter of children

the smile of delight...the mother's wit ...the mother within

the bible says see the root of the matter is found in me(job19:28)...

so it's not your father's approval that will carry you through

the inner strength ...the power within...the source

the Most High is the redeemer, the rock of the daughters of the world.

be strong, break down the walls drop the baggage,

take a stand, he is just a man ...you need your own approval, praise and applause.

if only to stop being lonely,

stop the fight and live the life you are meant to have

and daughters of the world be full time mothers to your girls...

stop the fight and live the life...the life you are meant to live

for you must know that your father does love you ...

he loves in his own special undocumented way...

without the applaud, the appraisal, the outward approval and

with out him and you ever tangibly knowing for any multiple of reasons

so stop the fight and live and love the life you are meant to have....

4–_HOW DO YOU FEEL_

How do you feel ...feel good like clouds and wind churning up the butter of the

sky, leaves fluttering on the trees, twirling, twisting, swaying, waves of the ebb

tide glistening bubbles, like twinkling stars...like watching ants and worms

dance and grass grow.. and the sun setting... wind whistling...listening to

silence and day dreaming...experiencing the inhale prior to the exhale...

savor the smile, indulge the laughter, radiate the positive, suck in the energy,

bask in the warmth of the moment...

how do I feel...feel with the mind, the reality of life, the comfort of the thought,

the essence of living, breathing, thriving, surviving the rat race of it all.

appreciating the good, the sensuous, not seeing the ugly and the bad,

not energizing the negative...

love gives flame heat ...fame to the positive and shame to the negative.

how do I feel

close to yet separate from ...free and independent from the all, part of the

whole and removed from the all...watching from the wings, yet being in the

midst, whirling, swirling in the turbulance of being actively at rest...

how do I feel...when I don't feel anything at all.

5–_LIGHT IN THE DARKNESS_

Like a feather floating in the air

like a whisper on the wind

like a ride into the sunset

like the ebb of the tide

like the curve of the rainbow

like the rustle of the leaves on the trees

like the rising of the sun

like the smell of the sea

like the call of the wild

we chase the illusive butterfly

the dreams of tomorrow

the nightmares of the past

the lost of the now the inconceiveableness of forever

the feel of the smell

the smell of the touch

do we get it all wrong...

trying to make it correct

the making of it destroys the creativeness

the uniqueness

the beauty

the reality of it

the evolution of it

like taking the shine of the sun

like taking the wet of the water

like taking the touch from the caress

like taking the taste from the smell

and the smell from the taste

like taking the swallow from the drink

like taking knowledge from the wisdom

we chase the illusive butterfly

whose life / existence is minute

thus we seek only the light in the darkness...

6–_IT STANDS TO REASON MY DEAR_

It stands to reason my dear

why boy hates girl

why winter opposes summer

why fish swim, birds fly

why east meets conflict

when west gets involved

why hell freezes over

and heaven closes its pearly gates

why fingers touch and ears hear

why there was jonah and the whale

and noah and the ark

the mouse scares the elephant

why eyes see

why tongues taste

it stands to reason my dear

that highs reflect lows

the kiss of death seals love and life

the downtrodden needs to be built up

and the big head can't see the ground

and so it stands to reason my dear

why I don't want you around...

7–DELICIOUS BUDDIES MAKE ME SMILE

Lucious buddies make me smile

hold my hand for just a little while

focus my attention on your smile

your wiggle and your style

aiming my center of attention at

the core of what I am looking fore

a moment of your sunshine while

looking at you from behind

shelter from the rain

as I stand in your shadow

clarity as I look at the twinkle in your eyes

protection in the strength of your embrace

laugther at your attempts of funmaking

royality as you prop me on a pedestal

lucious buddie make me smile

hold my hand for just a little while

feel like venus among the stars

as you profess your love for me

with lines I have heard all before...

you are like an aphrodisiac

a cool glass of wine .

a swim in the ocean

oysters on the half shell

strawberries dipped in chocolate

naked bodies glistening with oil

luscious buddies make me smile

hold my hand for just a little while

I mix safety and sexy all together

with the twist of your wrist

I live in the moment not giving

value to all your slip and slide

nor the ego you hide behind

lucious buddies make me smile

hold my hand for just a little while

as i focus my attention at the core

of what i am looking fore...

turkey gobble shift and shame

we both know this is just a game

let's ride this mile out all the same

lucious buddies make me smile

knowing there is no future

all the while...

8–_COLD_

Cold that ain't got nothing to do with the weather

nothing to do with disease

nothing to do with pain, runny nose, running away, cold

cold with fear, loss, death...

cold closes the throat, waters the eyes,

aches the head, sours the stomach,

cold realizes the fear,

shortens the breath,

pains the back,

cold in death for life is warm

cold in death for life is warm

cold in relationships for love is warm

cold in tears for smiles are warm

cold in weather for summer is warm

cold in stagnation/procrastination for fraction is hot

hot like going to the spa or a night at the bar

being bold enough to do the hot

when there is ever a breeze of the cold

is keeping it warm...

9–_BEGINNING OF THE END_

It is the beginning of the end of this love affair

not because the trust is gone

not because the lies are too long

not because the smile is not there

and the laugther has turned to a sneer

not because your feelings are elsewhere

not because your body is away from here

and your arguments are unfair

and you lose ability to share

and whatever I say you just don't hear

not because your love has turned to hate

even toward the food on the plate

not because you call me outta my name

and try to defame...

not because your stride isn't bold

and there's no tight to your hold

and your stare is cold

it is all about the slap

that I can't give you no slack

we use to ride out a storm

but not this form of abuse

you let loose...its put a noose in our love

and choked its life away from here

it's the beginning of the end of

this love affair 'cause you can't

stay here or anywhere near

living in fear is the one thing we can't bear

so go somewhere away from here my dear

because it's the beginning of the end

of this love affair !!!

10–_TODAY_

Finding my way while losing my way

I don't want to feel loss today

I want to be found today

I don't want to have a need for love

I want to be loved today

I don't want to wander around aimlessly today

I want a sense of direction and purpose

not the sense beat into me,

since it's really tenderness I seek

am I attracting loneness, sadness, feelings of desparation

I need to be needed today

I need to be needed today

will you feed my hunger

quench my thirst

stroke my ego

allow me to let go and fall into security

walk in faith

let my fears escape

hold onto the rainbow

ride out the curve

make a big splash

let the sparkling diamonds burst into the air

wetting up and dripping down the canvas of life

illuminating the horizon

brightening the future

warming the now

making hot love to the very fabric of the earth

falling into the depths

ripping holes of happiness

into the craters of life

no fisticuffs for us

just love from above

will you make my day ...today

11–_LONELY_

I got two eyes two ears two nares two legs

two arms two sets of chambers to my heart

and two ways to make love passionate and platonic

just waiting for you to get on it

a nickel for a pickle in days gone past

a penny for each question asked

if I said I love you to those when I passed

and didn't turn up my nose

at those that needed a second glance

I wouldn't be here lonely today

judging folks on a scale all mine from one to nine

weighed with baggage from those

that had taken advantage in early times

believing being cute and girlie is all I thought

had class not realizing those things too shall pass

and my youth won't last

wouldn't be here lonely today

trying to find my way

been through the thugs and seems that was fun

wth the excitement and drama trying to be mama to each

know nothing know it all

thinking I was having a ball

instead of being with the geek

and his stink feet, whose only call outside my name

would be honey I'll wash the dishes in the sink

or honey what do you think...

he would be doing the expected and life wouldn't be so hectic

in years gone by I thought the mundane was a shame

I cried I want to live my life my way

till I am found lonely this day

and my nerves all a fray

where's the ugly one too tall too fat too poor too short???

I need him today if only for moral support

where's the one that didn't drink,

didn't smoke, didn't take dope

and was the delight of my folks

he wanting to get married and settle down my life

I ran the other way

like I hadn't done everything twice

now I got to face this fight alone and with fright

advertising in personal columns

I got two eyes two ears two nares two legs

two arms two sets of chambers to my heart

and two ways to make love passionate and platonic...

just waiting for you to get on it...

12–THE BEAUTY OF NO PAIN - HAPPINESS

When the pain is so great

that you banish the feeling

to rebuke the pain/anguish/

fear/doubt/hurt/torment...

and when you cannot bear to feel any more

...numbness arrives

you reach for the pain

locate it - to stop it...

only to find you do not feel pain

no pain comes... no hurt

questionable happiness prevails

...endures - the beauty of no pain

the numbness that comes

when your pain is another persons pleasure

the reality leads to no pain

the beauty of no pain

and the happiness that comes

with the knowledge of the death of pain

the half cup

the birth of happiness

the grave is dug the cup runneth over and

the two dimensions become one

and the smile is engraved

tears no more..

13–A FRIEND FOR THE NIGHT

Sometimes you just need a friend for the night

hold me tight and make the world feel right

invade my inner sanctum

fireworks explodes

volcanoes erupts

lightning strikes

reality is super - induced

the universe evolves

hold me tight and make the world feel right

for sometimes you just

need a friend for the night

relinquish my rights to all your might

surmount yielding to overwhelming fright

as we succumb to the feelings of emotional reelings

for sometimes you just need a friend for the night

hold me tight and make the world feel right

surrender might ...indulge for a night...

lose control... as power takes hold ...

saturate the void... grasp the imaginary

annihilate the trepidation...

vanquish the mundane...

be spontaneously emancipated...

never ever the same...

hold me tight

with all your might

and make the world feel right...

for sometimes you just need

a friend for the night...

14–MELANCHOLY

I reach down deep to the inner most parts of my heart,

to find out what is tearing me apart.

need I suffer so desperately?

can I free myself of such bewilderment

rooted in the phantoms of my heart

tunnels of desperation

torrids pools of torment that twist,

turn and toss me topsy - turvy...

as my externals smile my inners are racked

with the excruciating agony of discomfiture

fighting with a heart that seems to be

in private arbitration with the devil,

as my outers laugh...

while feverishly trying to

suppress tyrannical screeches

created by the atrocious,

diabolical wrenching of my heart

you sit back manipulating

my heart as if it were

a marionette dancing

and spinning to the jealous

twitching of your aristocratic thumb

is this sadistic ceremonial rite

a part of some scenario

to build my endurance or

a prerequisite to the taming of the shrew

then again, would the credit of my

metamorphosis be fairly

placed on your shoulders or

would that just add to your vanity...

nay, the honor is not yours

you may be the stimulator

but never the administrator

of such pandemonium...

nay, I must look nearer

to find the the crux of

my melancholy....

15–_EGO TRIPPING_

He asked me did I miss him and I said yes

he asked me did I need him and I said yes

he asked me did I love him and I said yes

he asked me did I want him and I said no

no I don't want you

if you have to ask do I miss you

no I don't want you

if you have to ask do I need you

no I don't want you

if you have to ask do I love you

you can see by my eyes that

I love you

you can feel by my touch that

I need you

you can tell from my embrace

that I miss you

no i don't want you 'cause

your asking tells me

this is not love you're in...

it is an ego trip you are on

you may think that you love me

but you don't

you may think that you are

infatuated with me,

but ... you're not

no I don't want you...

you might even miss my missing you..

when I am gone

you might need my needing you

when I am gone

you might even hate my loving you

when I am gone

'cause the ego be's that way...

the ego wants

the ego needs

the ego misses

but the ego doesn't give...

the ego doesn't love

so no I don't want you...

16–*JUST OUT HAVING A DRINK*

yeah sam play it again

yeah sam play it again

play that down home funky blues

play that song about that no good man

play that song about that no good woman

yeah sam play it again

so I can go home and beat my

woman for things you say she did

and I can fantasize

about the things you say I did

yeah sam play that down home funky blues

so I can be part of the

world we are all supposed

to come from...

and

yeah sam let me have one more drink

and

yeah sam play that down home funky blues...

17–AND THE MOON REMAINS

When the need was there

I raped the moon

I basked in the moonlight

and smiled...

taken into its confidence and

questioned it 'til my needs

were satisfied

and smiled...

I raped the moon when the

need was there...

and the moon remains

unchanged....

18–*THE LAST LAUGH OR A COMICAL TRAGEDY*

It would be a comedy

if the tragedy was not so great

that lives of perfection

should exhibit so much defection

is it the apex or base that

deceives the balance or is it

the ideological balance that led

to its toppling

                disintegration

                        erosion of

that which is baseless

too much caring...overindulgence

in caution or the aggressive

blocking of movement to and fro

lack of flow or an unnoticed

washout like an ebb tide

like dawn to dusk

like a short time prior to a long time

like a long time prior to a short time

neither here nor there

up nor down...spring nor fall

sweet nor bitter

    beginning nor end

more likely the end of a great beginning

with its center a sobering plateau

above a warm valley, whose detail free simplicity

centers it complexity

those that laugh first and last

will cry longest as the joke is recognized

of this tragedy that is smiled away as a comedy

like the one that makes

a musical...a drama

an adventure... a satire

the customer... the salesman

the patient... the doctor

the victim... the perpetrator

the listener... the speaker

the dancer... the song

the treasure... the trash

the evening... the dawn

the prayer... the testimony

of this comedy

    that allows us

to hear the tragedy of silence

and realize the beauty of

bringing light to the darkness

of the tragedy/comedy

　　　　of too much said...

19–I LEFT MYSELF BEHIND

I left myself behind when I took my vows

I left myself behind when I had a child

I left myself behind when I put my family first,

the career, the parties, the character, the clothes, the soul,

the travel, the friends, the laughter, the dreams, the goals,

the mornings after...to do things later and before I die

funny to you my opinion used to qualify and you have even taken my side

I left myself behind to be by your side

that meant my intelligence had to hide

and the family became my only pride

like the pill the morning after my life is all shattered

waiting to see what you will do

from one moment to the next while deciding

the car, the house, the job, the school,

the other woman...

now you've gone too far

for you've taken the money from the cookie jar

I left myself behind letting you decide

every half baked idea that took us from here to there

and ending up nowhere

I left myself behind on a shelf

and that even caused me ill health

the arthritis that came when I found out

the situation wasn't as right as I thought

the headache when I didn't make you put on the brakes

and stop it all

the blind eye when I didn't want to see you fall

the pain in my side when I had to compromise my belief

like being robbed by a thief

the deaf ear when I could hear no more

of I'm wrong never right,

the gray hair when things were

no longer black nor white

you couldn't decide right from wrong

trying to justify things with a song and a dance

thinking romance would give us another second chance

the paranoia as I began to fill with fright

when money was tight

and you didn't come home till all hours of the night

I left myself behind sitting on a shelf

collecting dirt and wallowing in hurt

losing direction while running after promised affection,

love and happiness, a full nest and all the rest of the mess

I left myself behind hoping to find a new secure place in time immediate gratification was not my aim...

neither the hall of fame

but some deluded happiness all the same

instead of this misable shame of missing the train

and losing it all without even knowing

whence came the fall...

if you tell the tale it was me that was frail

chasing my tail that was never there to disappear

I left myself behind in books

and dreams and the many love scenes

that excited us when we were little boys with toys

and little girls with pearls in a beautiful world

of blue skies, green grass, red roses,

and a silver moon that sets too soon,

where rainbows and stars twinkle

and sunshines and fish swim and flowers grow

and time slows and I became someone

I don't know...

I left myself behind and I lost my mind

20–<u>TO DO OR NOT TO DO</u>

there are those that will do you

and those that you may want to do first

there are those that will have your back

through thick and thin with no strings attached

the gift is knowing who's who...

respecting that and giving slack

but not biting off the hand that feeds you

and rubs your back

knowledge is knowing when to do who

as well as who to do when...

not cutting off your nose to spite your face

for life is a long race that rooted in trust,

who to trust, what to trust, when to trust,

finding out how trusting you are

is really rising the bar

hold me near and dear to your heart

i am not the enemy with me you can be free

it is the tree that gives oxygen

the clouds that give rain

the brain that stores knowledge

and gives credibility to the sane

which is minimally defined as

what, where, when, how and why

you do anything and anyone...

21–_SKIN_

be it the wrapper,

coating, protective covering,

shell, defense/fence

be it thick or thin

sturdy...frail...opague

transparent...light...dark

colorful like christmas decor

icy cold, unfeeling, snowlike

or sunny bright color of summer,

earth colors, rainbow colors,

colors of the trees...of the sky

all lead us to the question of

why...

for protection, for warm

for difference, for binding

holding it all together

for color, for feeling,

for fences/defenses

22–ROOTS...STEP OUTTA THE TRAP

I must talk of what was/is

I must talk to you my love

talk to my love

ask you how do you get to

push buttons ... back against the wall

how did you lose your integrity,

ideals and principles...

your ability to smile

your faith in mankind

your passion for life

which drop in the bucket

what was the trigger

the straw that broke the camel

that makes you throw y o u

to the wind...test your faith in God

the world, the you!!

how did you get over the fence

break down the wall

separate the men from the boys

the good from the mediocre,

the shaft, the husk, the trash,

you must know that nothing changes

the root or the conscience fails

removes the soul, destroys the spirit

regardless of the dance,

the music and the melody...we leave the road

when the obstacles get too big

to go over, under, around

personal torture can't hurt

unless you feel ...

how do you get to paint the picture

lose the good ...the pure

that which you are sure

the anger, the pain,

the inability to explain,

you can't recognize

you don't want to see

to deny the senses

to refuse to cry

to hang by a thread

not knowing the alive

from the dead...

not warm, not cold,

not needing, not wanting,

not eating, not sleeping

no fear of death

no love of life

things dissappear / reappear

outta sight, outta mind

taste, tasteless

neither here nor there

the root runs deep to find the water

the source, the straight

the narrow...

back to center of the road

only if you are strong

no it was the weakness that

brought you along

drowning, suffocating, struggling

to reset your life

justify strife

long suffering, self -sacrificing

to provide credentials for your fight

but know that the root does not deviate

its route to the source is straight

follow the lead, come back to center

stop fighting the war

that does not exist

loose the bandages

unchain the monkey

unpaint the picture

end the battle

you are your only enemy

the back, the wall, the war,

the front, the facade,

it is yours ...the y o u

you don't know, don't want

don't recognize

start again on a new road

the old road straight

no longer narrow, running deep

an easy climb back to center

embrace integrity, ideals, principles,

love, life and all that was once

your boss, the leader, the rock,

your sparrow, the focus, the strength

the love that was never lost...

oppression, depression, fades away

don't question, don't ask, don't analyze

don't energze that segment of no life

the trap...

there is no turning back to it

the escape, the run, the return

the rebirth - born again-

the life, the living, the new beginnings

of the once that was ...

23–_IF YOU LOVE ME_

If you love me would it make me see clearer

would it make the world dearer

would it make me treat others fairer

would your love be a sunblock

an eye opener...perk up my system

and despel depression

replace my chaos for inner peace

and serenity...

bring me up eliminating my down

sending me in a spin all around

confusion giving way to false illusion

of eutopia...

if you love me do i gain the drunken

serenity that comes with mesmerization

the fantasy of youth revisited

the vulnerability of surreality

making me open to the belief

that not only birds fly...

if you love me will you give me flight delight and excite......

24–*WHY I LOVE YOU*

I love you because I can talk to you

about anything unless it's important

you are too close and everyone else is too far off

your needs are my needs

your wants are my wants

I won't tell you...'fore you should know

but I forgive you ...if you don't know

you don't know because ...I didn't tell you

so I forgive you for not knowing and acting appropriately

we smile to protect each other from

knowing and if we let something slip

we laugh like it was a joke

or it wasn't said at all

we'll pull together and push away

staying separate and together

no two people could be closer

to each other while apart

we know nothing about each other

yet I can feel your pain, sadness, and joy

without being near you

these are all daily emotions

that you deal with...however

you never say anything about your problems

your personal experiences

yet I know you... you know me

we confide in each other

without telling each other

anything that's important

no specifics, nothing personal,

no negatives...

that's why I love you

it's all known not said

understood, not revealed,

felt, not expressed

we tell each other about the

extended family

never our immediate family

there we stay closed mouth

while we keep the extended family and

friend's life an open book...

we feel we're being honest with each other

keeping each other in the loop

but we know it's just idle conversation

to keep us together...close while apart

we dream of each other at night...

nothing exotic... it's just our way

of letting each other know

I'm okay, if you're okay

we let each other believe

how wonderful our lives are going

a facade that keeps us going and

makes each other happy for each other

hoping, knowing and not knowing...

yet sure and certain and confident

that nothing in life or death

can break the connection

it's our bond

see that's why i love you

because i can talk to you about anything

and you can talk to me about anything

...unless it's important

25–<u>GET GROUNDED</u>

Let's hopscotch through life

not stepping on the cracks

that break our mother's back

miss the pitfalls, climb the mountains

swim the rivers, plant the gardens

breathe the air, learn to share

turning the other cheek won't make you weak...

the first straw didn't break the camel

but the last step completed the mile

half full is by far better than half empty

but there's still room for perfection

the forward of life is not going backward

and a yes beats a no

up will bring you from the down and

love will put your feet on the ground

26–_DON'T DO IT_

If you can't tell in good conscience

what you want to do... don't do it

if you can't tell your mom..don't do it

if you can't let her find out..don't do it

if you know she would say no ...don't do it

if the ancestors would frown upon it ...don't do it

if you don't want it thrown in your face

twenty years from now ...don't do it

if your job, friends, school and

church won't agree...don't do it

if the only person that goes along with you

is your best friend when it's wrong

know that's not your best friend and

...don't do it

know that what you are doing is surely

the preparation to lose your reputation

be willing to do the time for the crime

for it will surely bite you in the behind

if not now ...later

if you have to justify it...don't do it

if someone ask you to do something

that is not in the best interest of all

don't do it

if it don't come out in the wash

it will show up in the rinse

probably sooner than later

sooo... don't do it

what comes around goes around

because life ain't no sneak around...

life ain't played underground

so if you don't want it to come to light

don't do it

27–*THIS TOO SHALL PASS - GROWING PAINS*

Fear makes you slap your moma

yell at the kids ...pitch a fit

kick the dog... punch the wall

stomp the floor... slam the door

before you admit fear

just plain scared loss of control

brink of stress... full out frustration

is kicking your butt ... wringing your neck

making you not give a heck create a scene...

act the fool ...hey you might even quit school

no limit to the gimmicks

you try anything...but out and out cry

you can't be any less effective

open to sugggestions that don't make sense

with the situation only getting worse

at its best ...can't tell you nothing

'cause you sure you know something

can't figure what ... that's

why its changed your luck...

and what you're doing

just confirms you can't make the cut

settle down touch the ground

patience and tolerance should abound...

that is where the answers are found

don't even frown

you made yourself the clown

doing things that were unfounded

only showed people that you weren't

grounded...sure glad that time

goes fast ...for believe it or not

this to shall pass!!!

28–*LET IT BE*

Let it be let it be

when you stayed out one night

my friends said don't fuss and fight

let it be let it be wait and see

when the bills came up short

and you was not fired...they said

let it be let it be wait and see

when the holidays came, it was the same

you wasn't home for some lame explain

they still said

let it be let it be wait and see

now you always tired and back outta

whack...i'm suppose to believe

you work hard and all that

friends say just give you some slack

they still said

let it be let it be wait and see

you got a new car, but can't drive us far

talking about gas prices

my driving fast, hurting your car

still hear them saying

how good you are...

let it be let it be wait and see

however something about this

don't set right with me

so to all my friends

whom I love and cherish

who love to say

let it be let it be wait and see

well today I am waiting to see

the let it be let it be

that's been sucking the life outta me

Section II: Life

29–<u>LIFE</u>

It all happens too soon

sometimes the end is as

powerful as the beginning

for we always come full circle

and the beat goes on

for it's the memories that we thrive on

may the transistion be smooth

for it all happens too soon

longevity is in the memories

not the big bang and boom

30–<u>LET THERE BE MEANING TO LIVING</u>

Let there be meaning to living

don't just dance on my parade

without reason, rhyme nor rhythm

without cause nor effect

without giving a heck

you make me a wreck

just cause you suspect

you can win a bet

let there be meaning to living

substance without cause is a definite loss

where there is breath without breathing

the heart takes a beating

where there is no meaning

there is no fill to the needing

destiny, goals, and relationships

run cold, evil is bold and real life

can't take hold, like water without a bowl

let there be meaning to living

bite into the apple and learn

right from wrong...

life is so much more than a song

and things have to have value to go wrong

shame is just another way of saying pain

when reputation is the aim

let there be meaning to living

give a defined place for each space,

more than a notion of proportion

exist with some caution don't jump

into the fire following each novel desire

like life has no more attire then a car for hire

like taking action without acknowledging reaction

opposite in direction and equal in reflection...

leading to all types of rejection

yes back at you from you

let there be meaning to living

like an undercurrent of the ebb tide

you don't tire of things inadvertantly and repeatedly tried

songs in the wrong key of 'g' don't fulfill any needs

don't free up the feet

don't float the heart

don't give life a start

let there be meaning to living

dive into the pool and start swimming

uptake this race and make your mistakes

celebrate the mundane

don't just quiet the peace

sing the song...true things can go wrong

but fight for the right

keeping success in sight

plan your party

don't feed off of mine

the desire for the divine is more

than just in the mind

it's all about the giving

more than the getting

that is the best way to let there be meaning to living

yes it's all about the giving and caring

not fearing but sharing....

31–LIFE...IT'S JUST SOUP

The soup had a little of everything

little noodle, little rice, other things

that also seemed quite nice

the beans and tomatoes with

parsley thrown in sparsely

with a little carrot, onion, and garlic too

little more chicken then there was beef

and much water that taste like

it was from the street...

I believe the cook when he said

he put his foot in it and would also believe

he had hoof and mouth disease

it would taste the same hot or cold

you might just find it harder

to detect that it was old...

the soup had a little of everything

in it that's good and bad

all the aspect of life and strife

warm it up...cool it down

chew the bones, throw in bread and crackers too

stir it up and sip it down awhile

it will pull you through a little sickness

little health, little sadness, little happiness,

all the things in your life and strife

little affection, little friendship,

a little rejection, a little hatred

everything that will give you a rise

depending on how you visualize

the exact recipe is a little of everything

a little at a time, balanced in perfection

with love and protection

that's the beauty of soup

that's the beauty of life

a little of everything put together just right

32–*ME MYSELF AND I AM*

Sometimes we think the world is coming to an end

sometimes we fear there is nowhere from here

sometimes we feel the bottom has fell out

sometimes we say why me

we just cannot see why not me

sometimes time stands still

sometimes the walls close in

sometimes we can't see pass the trees

sometimes we feel we're in a dream

but crying won't wake us up

sometimes we want to curl up in a ball and

keep away from it all... while screaming

silently and hoping some one will stop this fall

we plead with God about giving our all

if he just take us off this fast rolling ball

we promise the world if someone will stop

this downward swirl...

we protest that we are good people

and list the good things we have done

and assure ourselves the bad wasn't that bad

if we remember any wrong at all

we don't deserve money problems

we give at the office and to beggars on the street

we don't deserve a broken heart

we love everybody and smile at the good bad and ugly

we don't deserve this dis-ease

we eat right and exercise sometimes

and express sympathy for the sick and dead and

sincere empathy for everyone's problems in between

heard about, read about or seen...

how could the world be this mean

we want to hate and hurt everything sight unseen

equal the playing ground and release pain all around

we even hate oneself and try to pinpoint causes of

this fate that only brings on a sadness that's too great

depression would be a better compared to this state that

we can find no expression for and can't escape

anger finally gives us a rise as we realize that

we have the choice to make things fine...if we

decide to fight this fight instead of flight

no where to go, so we better put on a good show

if it's to be it's up to me myself and i

we'll have to focus, set goals and see

trials and tribulations are just challenges to me

another mountain to climb, road to ride not somewhere

to run and hide... we can do this

God will send us what we need

just don't let the fear feed

fight the feelings to look back, make plans for the future

claim not to be the mortar be the inspiration

not the sick but the well, the survivor not the dead

live and be alive not poor us, rich us

it's not the night, it the day of our life

the light and darkness represent a newday

that the lord has made let's rejoice in it

we are not hungry we're full of experience

we're not sad it's glad we want to bring out

run and shout ... that's what it's about

think on those things that's good

that's what the bible says we should and

have the strength of a mustard seed that's us

we ain't alone and where two agree

it's the good we will see

our Lord teaches us, stretches us

strengthens us,we are workers of the Lord

the work seems hard but it goes with the job

onward till the task is complete

we ain't recognizing no defeat

we just getting better every day in every way

the devil's a liar, we in the Lord's hire

the Lord's our motivator and provider

we are energized and no ways tired

we are going to keep on going until we beat out

this fire ...the sun won't set on us

we'll make it rise again like after rain

the sun will shine like after darkness

there's light ...thus sometimes you think it's a hard fight

however that's the way we fight hard to win

it is now or never that's the game we in

no time to wallow in self pity

been there did that and it's not pretty

we in it to win it

we ain't itsy bitsy we bigger than that

sometimes life seems like a slap

but we come back strong cause we are more than a song

strong cause we ain't what's wrong

strong so we can carry on

sometimes we slip but we ain't whipped

far inside we know that sometimes ain't all times

we let ths situation know that

this too shall pass cause we are in this

together and ready to whip ass

we vow to be the healthiest, smartest, wealthiest, happiest

we can be for if it's to be it's up to we

and this situation nor any other won't

beat, defeat, or define the me, myself and i'm

i dig deep into my all time infinite sea of God's love

and pull out peace love joy and self approval

that allows me to win 'cause the me...myself...

and I define the I am that I am that I am

33–_I KEEP MY EYES ON HEAVEN_

I keep my eyes on heaven above 24-7

I keep my eyes on heaven around the clock

'cause his love will never stop

when i'm asleep or awake

eating steak or taking a break

I am mesmerized by his love

I keep my eyes on heaven 24 - 7

I keep my eyes on heaven around the clock

'cause his love will never stop

count the ways he shows his love

he pays my bills even when I am ill

he feeds me till I get my fill

he fixes me up when I am sick

his love made me well real quick

I owe my prosperity, health

happiness and success to his love

I don't know what other people are thinking of

I keep my eyes on heaven 24 - 7

I keep my eyes on heaven around the clock

'cause his love will never stop

he designed me to perfection and than gave me protection

so he got all my affection

I keep my eyes on heaven above 24 - 7

I keep my eyes on heaven all around the clock

'cause his love will never stop

they say make a joyful noise to the Lord

I say the Lord's name is a joyful noise

to my ears and washes away all my fears

I'm down here but my heart's up there

I keep my eyes on heaven 24 - 7

I keep my eyes on heaven all around the clock

'cause his love will never stop

through thick and thin i know i'm going to win

as long as I believe in him

I keep my eyes on heaven above 24 - 7

I keep my eyes on heaven all around the clock

'cause his love will never stop

I count my blessings morning night and noon

'cause some things you can't do too soon

it's better than being born with a silver spoon

God's my gold and i am standing bold

the Lord has taken hold

I keep my eyes on heaven above 24 - 7

I keep my eyes on heaven all around the clock

'cause his love will never stop

the devil can push and shove

but I'm no way moved from his love

my strength is from the Lord above

I keep my eyes on heaven above 24 - 7

I keep my eyes on heaven all around the clock

'cause his love will never stop

in hot or cold when i'm strong or weak

be it light or dark, awake or asleep

in bondage and free he's been with me

allowing me to see and keeping joy and estasy in me

I keep my eyes on heaven above 24 - 7

I keep my eyes on heaven all around the clock

'cause his love will never stop

everyone take a stand and raise your hands

the Lord is definitely the man

he gave us every grain of sand

and breath of air and the eyes to look and stare

so I keep my eyes right there...

I keep my eyes on heaven above 24 - 7

I kee pmy eyes on heaven all around the clock

'cause his love will never stop

34–<u>CAN'T FIND NO REASON NOT TO LOVE YOU</u>

Can't find no reason not to love you

from the inside out and all about

can't find no reason not to love you

when my bills come the money is there when due

can't find no reason not to love you

when my love one died you was by my side

and brought me through

can't find no reason not to love you

when the house burned down

you brought me a new one

can't find no reason not to love you

when the car broke down

you got me to work without a scar

can't find no reason not to love you

when they pulled my tooth

you made sure it didn't hurt

and I could still chew

can't find no reason no to love you

when the boss retired

I was still hired

can't find no reason not to love you

when the food ran out

you filled my mouth

can't find no reason not to love you

when I was alone you was my friend at home

can't find no reason not to love you

I won the case when I went to court

knowing it was you that fought

can't find no reason not to love you

when I got sick you made me well quick

can't find no reason not to love you

from the hair on my head to the nails on my toes

I know I'm the one that you choose

can't find no reason not to love you

awake or asleep I don't feel no defeat

for you have my soul to keep

can't find no reason not to love you

with you in my heart

I get no ways tired

I know I can walk on fire

so devil my soul is not for hire

can't find no reason not to love you

you are my defense against all the rest

can't find no reason not to love you

you are always here so I have nothing to fear

winter summer spring and fall with my God I can do it all

can't find no reason not to love you

whatever you put me through I can do

can't find no reason not to love you

you didn't say it would all be good

but you promised you would see me through

and you have been true ...so

I can't find no reason not to love you

when I laid down and wanted to give up all

and drop dead ...I remembered

you had anointed my head

and restored my soul,

my spirit was lifted I knew why I existed

I can't find no reason not to love you

35–<u>HOW WE SURVIVE</u>

Love is what we yearn for

peace is what we fight for

quiet is what we listen to

beauty is what we see

touch is how we soothe the pain

cut grass after rain is what we smell

patience is what we learn

respect is what we earn

accountability is what determines character

responsibility is what we shoulder

pride is what makes us bolder

and as we get older and discard the other jive

we learn that taking care of one another

is how we stay alive and...

putting a side our differences is how we will survive

36–_CAN'T WAIT_

Can't wait till I win the lotto

going to buy me a house

going to buy me a big car

going to kiss that job good bye

my clothes going to be fly

going to get my mink coat

won't let nobody get my goat

can't wait to get me a husband

we going to travel the world

I am going to be his only girl

we going out nights and dance on the world

we going to get a king size bed

a pool table and dining room chairs

even going to have a chandelier

and a chaise lounge, won't wear no frown

can't wait till I retire

going to set this world on fire

going out every night till I get tired

won't take nothing from folks

going to sow my wild oats

stay up late drink and smoke

can't wait can't wait can't wait

can't wait oh heck no ...won't wait

time to make fantasy reality

stop excuses put offs and put ons

time to make hay while I still got days

waiting on the lotto like I'm chasing a carrot

delaying my dreams by any means and rotting away

waiting for the lotto

waiting for the husband

waiting for retirement

hell I will probably go broke,

be an old maid and get fired before that day

stop the madness, I'm just telling myself

I can't have it...waiting waiting waiting

making excuses so I don't mentally lose it

starting today i am going to change my ways

I am going to get me a house anywhere

on earth that's where I want to be

then go out and grab the first man I see

that's free... he can be old, ugly, fat and bald

but not funky..baby mama drama and all

it is fine...he is mine

plenty of them out there

scared of rejection

saying they don't want commitment

because they been previously smitten

his attitude tells you he's been bitten

it is okay, I'll let you have your way

I am on a mission

I just want everybody to play their position

so I don't have to put a sign on

the bedroom door saying I am gone fishing

I am going to get that car any car

cause an ugly ride beats a pretty walk any day

and drive it far around the block

and back to where you are

let him put a ring on my finger

plain gold band ..ain't trying to compare diamonds

the ring is the thing I ain't never had

learn to be a happy camper

love what I earn

take my butt to work

glad I got somewhere to go

jaw-jive all day long

and home to my beau

eat my food and then we both travel

to the moon not a moment too soon

get my hair did, and my nails done

got my house, my man, my job

and a car traveling near and far

dancing to my music right where you are

waiting for the lotto

waiting for a man

waiting for retirement

no no no baby I am not loss I am found

'cause i finally got my feet on the ground

and turned this girl around

ain't no more gonna wanna coulda shoulda

waiting around...

37–THREE LITTLE WORDS

Why can't you say I love you

without getting tongue tied

without looking to the side

without waiting for me to cry

why can't you say I love you

'cause you don't mean it

or cause you don't know what it means

'cause it shows commitment

or 'cause you don't want commitment

'cause it breaks down walls

or 'cause you need to build up walls

'cause you feel it's expected

or 'cause it's not what you expected

did a one night stand

wind up with too many demands

you brought flowers,

we shared showers

now you get mad at things that made you glad

like cooking for your friends

or watching the game to the end

now my flirting seems to be hurting

why can't you say I love you

would it put an end to your world

or is there another girl

the fact that trees flower gives them their power

you see with your eyes the beauty of life

clarity comes with vision

you touch with your hand the softness of cotton

feelings palpate your heart from which life starts

hunger is fed by food that nourish the body

love touches the heart and makes life flourish

love puts pep in your step

smile to your frown

happiness in your heart

twinkle to your eyes

fills the gap

picks up the slack

gives you self worth

breaks down the walls

makes you whole

restores your soul

no valley too low

no mountain too high

there becomes a purpose

and the answer to why

why the earth turns

why the clouds form

why the waves break

why the sun warms

why the rain falls

why the ice melts

why the flowers bloom

why your kisses are like warm caramel

why smiles find my lips and eyes when I hear your name

and when I coo it, it's your road to fame

why can't you say I love you

and put macho-ism to shame

with romance being the blame

why can't you say I love you

those three little words

it doesn't define weakness or sweetness

it's trust without the fuss

caress without the arms

kisses without the lips lust you can trust

for those three little words

embrace you like a bear hug

like tender touches on your back

whispers in your ear

pinches on your hip

candy dripping from your lip

it's like the ballet of the nutcracker suite

and swan lake all in one

*like the fight of hearts in battle i*n the mid of night

I love you I love you I love you

why can't you say I love you

are the words too big

or the impact too great...

38–_WHERE ARE YOU ...WHERE ARE AM I_

I ask where are you... where am I

where is the beauty...where is the wonderment

the love and joy of life without you

there is the longing ...but no belonging

there is the quiet ...but no peace

there is the ease ...but it is not easy

there is heat ...but no warmth

there is food ...but no fulfillment

the sun sets ...but there is no settle down for the night

the stars like the sun shine without the twinkle

and brightness that differentiates day from night

sleep and wake becomes the same without the

highs and lows that come with an active heartbeat

the sadness ...the gladness

the open ...the close

the ups ...the downs

the ins ...the outs

the hot ...the cold

the wet ...the dry

the hunger of it all...

I ask where is the beauty ...where is the love

the joy ...the learning ...the yearning

the integrity of life...

the norms are strange to me

the strangeness now norm

no pain ...

just lack of feeling, wonderment, and belonging

part of the whole yet separate from it all

trust and faith and fear and doubt ...

play games with my sanity

discomfort sits where comfit sat

where is the beauty

    where are you

        where am I

39–<u>DAY AND NIGHT</u>

Day and night teaches you

two things ...to laugh and cry

laugh when there is hope

and cry when things seem hopeless

for these are lessons often used

in the days and nights of your life...

and we move from hope to hopelessness

sometimes as quickly as we move from

crying to laughter and very often

as smoothly as day and night

40–<u>NO LIFE / SUICIDE</u>

They

watch the

body for signs

of life

still

I lay

no one ever

thought me

life

of the

party or show

but still

cold

I lay

as they watch

for signs

dead

no life

curiously suddenly still

too much

love

too late

locked in death

I lay

41–AN EXTENSION OF HIS PERFECTION

I have seen life that evolved amazingly both in body and mind

I have seen life where the body is perfect and the mind doesn't catch up

I have seen life where the mind is perfect and the body doesn't catch up

I have seen life which has come and stayed for only a day, then gone away

I have seen life that stay and stay and stay, that's why I say

not my way but thine, all happens in a matter of time

a twinkling of time like stars shine

not all measureable in mind, for time is in positive

and negative memories that take us through highs and lows

of things we don't know, as God gives us a show and tell

at times it makes us feel like we going through hell

and all the while we doing well

as he stretches us he teaches us, to love what is put on our plate

he makes the dates, so don't fuss, just love and trust

God's here for us , he will show us the way

so continue to pray with delight

his shining light will distinguish our plight

he is doing what's best for all of us

not our way but thine all things will work out fine in due time

think on thngs that are good like he said we should

see the beauty, enjoy the gifts, release the if's,

cherish the love, bathe in his radience, learn the lesson

it's not just an expression that we are an

extension of his perfection....

42–NO THINGS WON'T BE THE SAME

Tender moments at the end of the day

that's all we got

tender memories are a whole lot

the smiles... the laughter

the hours after

the hugs, the kisses are the things

that's missing...

working together shoulder to shoulder

running in the park

laughing when the car couldn't start

burning the food and playing the fool

love games in the afternoon

stolen moments that end too soon

tender memories of waking up

in love positions and knowing

the last one up will wash the dishes

paying peter and ignoring paul

till the paychecks could cover it all

we had happiness that dispelled the fears

and other times we just didn't care

telling the kids how they shouldn't be frail

then letting them get away with murder

to prevent whipping their tail

and the times your family over stayed their

welcome even though they had been there

just an hour , keeping us from getting in the shower

you thinking you had all the power

shouting just to make us cower

all the while we laughing at your face looking sour

your attempts at cooking

and coming up with bright ideas

that I had given you will always draw a smile

as I compliment you all the while

and as you thank me for my support

instead of saying I told you so

I just praise you on your get up and go

tender memories of my hair styles gone wild

short, long, tipped, snipped, fried, dyed

and layed to the side...

but your crew cut, mohawk, bush, and

finally bald topped it all.

yes we kept smiling through it all

the winters with little heat

and the summers of little air

we had each other that's all we cared

no things won't be the same

as we hold on to the positives

forgive the negatives

smile as we run through the photos of

the good times in our mind

and hear the laughter of old times

no things won't be the same

but tender memories will erase the pain

and keep us from going insane...

43–_THE GREATEST FIND....NEVER LOST_

I lost my child, I lost my mother,

I lost my father, I lost my love

but how is that ???

I didn't find them on a doorstep

I didn't find them in the trash

in the seat on the bus while travelling north

or in a cracker-o-jack box

or a cereal food that fills my gut

not in the park where the trees were green

and grass was cut and the flowers bloom,

where the sunset is orange and the sky is blue

and the birds sing all in tune

near the pond where the small fish swim and

the old men talk of what coulda, woulda, shoulda been

how could I lose what wasn't mine to find

but a gift of God that I claim as mine

I didn't give them away so where did they go

to the mountain top, to the deep blue sea,

the rain forest or arid desert,

to the nine layers of hell

or thirteen levels of heaven

what kind of relationship did we have

that they didn't take me with them

for if they went by choice

they would surely have taken me

along cause our love was just that strong

then again was their mission/ their work/their job

complete and done ...did they work faster than me

and now waiting in the light for me to come

did i lose them or they leave for

all the good things they achieved

giving me love, giving me happiness,

giving me security, giving me hope,

giving me encouragement, giving me laughter

even in these sad moments after...

bringing smiles to my face for helping me

to keep pace with the rest of the human race,

seeing and appreciating the beauty

that before now had slipped away as i pushed

through the days not giving a hay.

did I learn the lessons that they were here

to teach me...to love, to care, to be fair,

so they had to say adeiu, adios,

goodbye my dear our job here is done

finally cleared ...

we return to God from which we appeared

sent as gifts on loan like a call on the phone

the pick up and the let down, the open, the close

the in my life abruptly, the out suddenly

fore me to live my life long and improved

by the golden rule, walking in faith

even through i believe it all happened too soon

I appreciate that i was not the controllor,

manipulator of my fate ...

I wasn't the reason they had to escape ...

it was the Lord that made the date, for them

to visit me and go back home to him

leaving me and all their kin...but in

the memories they left behind

there was a wonderful find

a set of crutches handmade

of their love to hold me up,

support me and let me know

they are by my side...

so I don't ever have to say goodbye

yes I just have to look around at things

I found for me and all to learn to give applaud,

graditute and thanks.

I found lovely things,

I found wonderful things,

I found beautiful things,

I found funny things,

I found dear things,

I found helpful things,

I found strong things that

helped me to remember them

on and on and in ways that

can never never be lost...

Section III:
Thoughts of Healing

44–*TO KNOW ONESELF*

To know oneself is to give oneself the gift of joy

the gift of freedom, the smell of reality

the love of self, to overcome fragility

to expell vulnerability

for strength is in the knowledge

truth, pride, wisdom, and gratitude

to know oneself is to give oneself

the gift of self-esteem, trust, pride and confidence that overcomes fear

for faith comes with the belief in self

the gift no one else can give you

is to know oneself...to hug oneself

to empower one self...to forgive oneself

to enjoy oneself...to truly know oneself is to love oneself

45–<u>DO WHAT YOU FEEL</u>

today is real

yesterday is done

tomorrow didn't come

today do what you feel

enjoy the big deal

today live your fill

if you don't

know that you performed the kill

life is one day at a time

make it an easy climb

take time to smell the roses, coffee and horses

smile as you walk every mile

look at life like a child

be real ...do what you feel

anger, worry and hurt only steal

the happy moments that are your just deserts

this is the day the lord has made

for you to rejoice in it ...

but you have a choice

you have a voice in it

sing and let the heavens ring

or cry until you die

and then look around and ask why

do what you feel

remember anger, worry and hurt

steal that which is real

a wonderful happy, awesome

life is the big deal

start now...start now

begin today that's what is real

the future is fantasy

the past is memory

today is real

live the big deal with all your heart

and all the tomorrows

will be ignited with the spark!!!

46–<u>GETTING THERE</u>

Winning is not the beginning

success is not the end

in perfection there is room for correction

and even a change of direction

it takes courage to persevere until you get there

wisdom is a desire

but for intellect you need a burning fire

that grows greater with each log

of knowledge you acquire

no mountain is unclimbable

no valley to low or deep

mountains are the height

valleys the depths

that you find in the extent

of the challeges you will meet

like burdens of every race

they only sting the face

they are only wear and tear

so no need to fear as the vision

becomes clear... you will get there

for the world is paved for all

that have faith and willing to run the

race, play their part it's an art

the game is not new for

the Most High is responsible for your design

he will see you through and make your

light shine...like a planet in the universe

he will show favor and make you first

in line and right on time

as stated in the bible verse...

he will get you there

sing a song when things seem to be going wrong

hum a melody like my sweet chick a dee

whistle a tone like this little light of mine

pat your foot to all is fine

clap your hands to something snappy

nod your head to don't worry be happy

do it like there's no hurry and don't worry

everyday for ten minutes

watch the grass grow

smell the ocean water

close your eyes and feel the wind blow

listen to the silence

wish on a star

pray for others

give thanks for self

mentally climb a mountain

successfully walk on fire

run a race and never tire

build a house and tear down

the retaining the walls

let the sky be the only limit

when you are in it to win it

every day for ten minutes and

appreciate and applaud what God has done

while you are having fun

and know that all the bumps are

only fair while getting there

47–THE RE-CREATION OF LIFE

To be in the re-creation of life

makes you want to take a chance

find romance

check with yourself to register in advance

all the feelings you have had

let the anger explode so you can lighten the load

let the joy fill the void and like your own noise

let the tears prepare you for all you

may hear as you frolic in the stares

as only a blindman would dare

be the drummer in your parade

and bang on the world

let the music resonate down to your soul

break dance in the rain

so you can make a big splash even though

you thought that was all in the past

being in the re-creation of life

makes you want to touch someone

when you think it's too much

and for you it's not enough

swim in the waters of life

drown in the undercurrents of happiness

float in the sky and let the clouds

caress you while drawing in the energy of the most high

redirect your thoughts to harness

the magnetic force of the center of the earth

and fill yourself with it for all it's worth

say nay to the hurts

de-energize all pain for preservation

of your mind frame

let the down flowing cosmic rays

fill your hunger...to quench your thirst

look for ways to increase your intellect

spin in the winds of the warm

breeze attracting hot love like

sun in the tallest trees or

or feel free and naked as the trees

that has loss its leaves

standing tall stripped bare

to face the froze

to be in the re-creatiion of life

you want to tap dance on the moon

so take the initative to be efficient

let the imagination run wild and achieve

whatever you can conceive

so the future is more than you

have ever believed or had before

to be in the re-creation of life

you just don't walk out in faith

you run the earth and solve all the hurts

you heal the wounded

you bring happiness to the sad

you feed the hungry

you plant the gardens

you smell the roses

you raise the sun and set the moon

and rejoice in every good thing

the lord has given to truly

appreciate the gift of living

in the re-creation of life you do it all

winter spring summer and fall

with a gusto that only a true believer

can musta

in the re-creation of life

the sea has no bottom and the sky has no limit

ahh to be in the re-creation of life is to live and love

take a chance for romance and check for

yourself all the feelings you have had ...

48–*REHABILITATION ...LEARNING TO WALK AGAIN*

It is like being spanked as a child

you brace yourself against the blows

cringe and bite your teeth

with each strike

finally you scream and cry and

the pain is no longer the point

as your attention is now

held by your own screams

and the process of executing

these screams

and like a child you live through it

and learn to walk again

rehabilitated...

49–SMELLING MY OWN COFFEE

Smelling my own coffee

focusing on me

it's all about me...

the warm...the heat...the passion

the calm...the cool...the comfort...

the strength...the depth

    the robustness of my coffee

focusing on me...the inner me

break down the walls

shed the skin

loose the boundaries

get to the core

there is only the strength

no weaknesses

there is only the future

no past

the now escapes before

we can get the word out

it's not about where I am

for life moves too fast...

I am already past being there

it is all about me as I

fumble... stumble...tumble

into my future

the real is surreal

drop the extraneous paraphernalia

it is not about the id

nor the ego

the smell of my own coffee

focuses on me

it is all about me

the energy, the aroma, the color

the warmth, the clarity

the unmistakable uniqueness

of the flavor of me

the smell of my own coffee...

focusing on me

lets my light shine

and awakens me...

50–EYES ON THE FUTURE, LET NO HURDLE BE DISARMING

Look back ...

    to respect and cherish

the past

look forward ...

    embrace life, love, imagination,

      fantasy and challenge with

        positive exhilaration, wonderment

        excitement and joy

let no hurdle be disarming ...

each moment a fabulous beginning

    to a lifelong beckoning,

      climb and race to perfection

        perfection...the ultimate apex

        reached only by those that live life

        with aggressive enthusiasm...

let no hurdle be disarming ...

as you live in present tense

    with your eyes on the future

      and the future a continuous

        spontaneous generation and regeneration

        an extravagant evolution and metamorphosis

let no hurdle be disarming

keep your eyes on the future ...

GLOSSARY

ABUSE- to dishonor, violate deceive injure, ill-treat, misuse, impose or insult, take advantage of another; verbally, physically, mentally, emotionally

COMPASSION – kindness, empathy, fellowship, a character trait that extends from the heart straight out with no strings attached combined with mercy gives life a rewarding meaning.

COURAGE – calm, cool, collected bravery in the face of obstacles, control of fear and confidence, it is the coming to the rescue, not the rescue, morally, valiantly and fearlessly.

DEATH – culmination of life's experiences can also be seen as the end of one stage, just prior to the beginning of another.

DEDICATION – faith with action, pledge of devotion, respect, honesty, and loyalty.

FAITH – optimism, one's personal inner positive reality, that which needs no proof but relies on trust and allows us to bear the pain and joy of life.

FRIENDSHIP – to have a friend is to be a friend loyally with affection, obligation, love, trust, positive criticism and reinforcement; the oneness that compliments each other with growth. The noblest thing a person can do is to be a friend with no strings attached.

HONESTY – genuineness, moral excellence expressed via one's integrity, cornerstone of love and success and friendship.

LIFE – a combination of experiences necessary for existence.

LOVE – dedicated affection and devotion, respect, honesty and loyalty, acting out of compassion, respect, gratitude, loyalty, accountability, and feelings of responsibility.

LOYALTY – allegiance, patience, resourcefulness, constancy, devotion, and love are ingredients within the pot of loyalty. The receiver of the pot feels friendship, security, comfort, and happiness.

LUST – *believed need for affection, desire for indulgence.*

OPPRESSION/PAIN – *feelings felt by the abused from the abuser can be fitted to the north from the south Vietnamese, the children of Israel from the ruler of the Egypt, East Indians from the Pakistanis, the Blacks from the Whites, the weaker from the bully, the employee from the employer, the feelings of powerlessness from the purposed powerful, can be claimed by every sector of human beings even girls from the boys, even Catholics versus the Protestants, etc.*

PERSEVERANCE – *sticking to your guns, hanging in there, discipline fortified with undying faith creating endurance that generates a system of success.*

PROCASTINATION – *root of failure, indecision, fear, doubt, stagnation, and undermining oneself.*

RESPONSIBILITY – *shouldering duties and obligation not viewed as burdens both big and small, it molds leaders and allows us to get along, mature and grow, a mix of self - discipline, accountability, dedication, reflection, and obedience.*

SELF-DISCIPLINE – *is what adversity blooms, it's the calm that proceeds / follows and prevents many a storm.*

WORK – *tedious, strenuous, exhausting drudgery – ones success is linked to attitude when viewed as a sense of responsibility, self- discipline, or an exercise in perseverance it can become a labor of love and life, a positive investment in self, the expending of energy for positive accomplishment, a means to a specific end.*

INDEX

(this index connects these expressions to the 50 poems, prose and glossary by the poem number)

compassion - 30, 44, 18, 23, 41, 33, 34, 35, 43, 46, 37, 5, 48

courage - 3, 1, 43, 45, 36, 46, 20, 39, 22, 49, 47, 41, 48, 5, 32, 35

death - 41, 42, 29, 4

dedication - 22, 32, 33, 34, 35, 43, 46, 49, 48, 50

faith - 5, 8, 45, 47, 42, 32, 33, 34, 43, 49, 48, 50

friendship - 1, 2, 24, 30

honesty - 9, 44, 18, 32, 46, 36, 37, 17, 48, 50

life - 3, 6, 9, 44, 10, 11, 18, 19, 20, 21, 22, 24, 31, 25, 26, 27, 47, 41, 42, 29, 32, 33, 34, 35, 46, 36, 37, 39, 49, 489, 50

love - 9, 1, 2, 23, 25, 41, 33, 34, 37, 48

loyality - 24, 25, 41, 33, 34, 35, 46, 48

lust - 7, 11, 13

oppression/pain - 4, 10, 12, 14, 40, 49

perseverance - 19, 49, 50, 22, 27, 47, 41, 32, 33, 34, 35, 46

responsibility - 3, 48, 16, 50, 45, 2, 22, 27, 32, 35

self-discipline - 27, 47, 44, 46, 45, 2, 48, 5, 22, 31, 35